Quotes
by NAD

NANA AWERE DAMOAH

DAkpabli

DAKPABLI & ASSOCIATES
ACCRA

QUOTES BY NAD

ISBN: 978-1542981934

Edited by James Anquandah (j.anquandah@yahoo.com)

Cover design and Book Layout by multiPIXEL Limited

P O Box ML 343, Mallam, Accra, Ghana

Email: multipixellimited@gmail.com

Tel: +233 302 333 502 | +233 201 578 865 | +233 246 725 060

Cover picture: Shirt courtesy GIGI by WearGhana,

photo by Kobby Blay Photography

Published by

Dakpabli & Associates

Accra, Ghana

Tel: +233 264 339 066 | +233 244 704 250

Email: DAkpabli.Readathon@gmail.com

Author's Contact: Nana Awere Damoah

Email: ndamoah@yahoo.co.uk

ALSO BY NANA AWERE DAMOAH

I SPEAK OF GHANA

TALES FROM DIFFERENT TAILS

THROUGH THE GATES OF THOUGHT

EXCURSIONS IN MY MIND

SEBITICALLY SPEAKING

NSEMPIISMS

Nana Awere Damoah was born in Accra, Ghana. He holds a Master's degree in Chemical Engineering from the University of Nottingham, UK, and a Bachelors in Chemical Engineering from the Kwame Nkrumah University of Science and Technology, (KNUST), Kumasi, Ghana. Nana spent all his secondary or high school years at Ghana National College, Cape Coast, Ghana and speaks fondly of growing up in the suburb of Kotobabi in the Ghanaian capital, where he started his education at the local Providence Preparatory School.

NAD, as he is affectionately called by his readers, is a British Council Chevening alumnus and an associate of Joyful Way Incorporated, a Christian Music Ministry in Ghana, where he was the group's National President from 2002 to 2004.

Nana started writing seriously in 1993 when he was in the sixth form and has had a number of his short stories published in the *Mirror* and the *Spectator*. In 1997, he won the first prize in the *Step Magazine* National Story Writing Competition. His writing has appeared in StoryTime ezine, Legon Business Journal, Sentinel Nigeria Magazine and the anthology, *African Roar* (StoryTime Publishing, 2010).

He is the author of six other books and has also contributed to two anthologies. He keeps two personal blogs at www.nanadamoah.com and www.nanaaweredamoah.wordpress.com.

He is married to Vivian. The couple and their children, Nana Kwame Bassanyin, Nana Yaw Appiah, and Maame Esi Akoah, are based in Tema, Ghana.

Dedicated to three friends of mine who pointed me to new ways of exploring my writing and continue to serve as sounding boards: Korklu Laryea, Kwabena Opoku-Agyemang and Kofi Akpabli.

CONTENTS

Section A	Government, Politics & Politicians	9
Section B	Wit, Fun & Satire	23
Section C	Love, Friendships, Family & Marriage	37
Section D	Ghana & Africa	43
Section E	Books, Learning & Reading	55
Section F	Nation Building	61
Section G	Proverbs & Sayings	81
Section H	Advice and Instruction	93
Section I	Social media	103
Section J	Life & Career	109
Section K	God & Religion	117
Section L	Passion & Dreams	123
Section M	Writing	126
Section N	Education	137
Section O	Leadership	141
Section P	Journalists & Media	145

SECTION A
GOVERNMENT,
POLITICS & POLITICIANS

A1.   The propensity for foot-soldier nonsense is no respecter of party colours.

A2.   The way we politicise the issue of drugs in Sikaman, one day, you will go to Mr Mark's drug store to buy abom-belt and he will ask you whether you are *osono* or *akatamanso* before selling it to you.

A3.   Many of our politicians think politics is only a game; refuse to play!

A4.   The shambolic takeover or transfer or merger or whatever we choose to call it between Ghana Gas and GNPC is symptomatic of many of the decisions and moves of this government. How come that even within the same family, agreements cannot be reached and executed with finesse? Why?

A5.   When politicians accuse themselves of various vices, pay attention: they speak the truth. The accusers and the accused are both guilty of same; either in the past or present.

A6.   Kufuor had his 50-cent moment. Mahama had his Montie moment. Years from today, both moments will define them.

A7.   Never let the politician think he can think for you.

A8.   Don't let politicians buy your mind for a pesewa.

A9.   Election campaign time is always a great time to calibrate logical capacities and capabilities.

A10.   Words spoken in response to initial words spoken and the spirit with which the responses were delivered will greatly influence this (December, 2012) election.

A11.   Our politicians insulted our intelligence each day and yet we smiled and said, "More please!" They told us to go to hell and we actually asked for advanced tickets. They took us for fools and yet, we praised them for their blessings.

A12.   Our politicians know you have the power to decide their fate. They know their real sizes. Sadly, citizens usually don't fully appreciate their power.

A13.   Why can't we give our politicians similar treatment football lovers served the Black Stars in the Uganda game? Surely, the Black Stars get the opportunity to do a Brazil fiasco every two or four years whereas the politicians do it daily. And, oh, I hold the politicians responsible for the Brazil debacle. Root-cause analysis.

A14.   Campaigning all of the time, governing none of the time. These are the days of our lives.

A15.   This foot soldiers-going-on-rampage-at-will nonsense must stop! One day, they will have nothing else to vandalise but their leaders, who have failed to call them to order today.

A16.   The Parliamentary vetting (of ministers) usually disbosoms a lot for me, especially why we are in this state of atrophy as a nation.

A17.   "Do you know what that amount of money can do?" The Ghanaian politician's favourite populist question. Never asked when he is considering his benefits, deserved or otherwise.

A18.   The Sikaman politician, as a first recourse, looks for whom to blame when trouble arises. If he doesn't find a ready excuse, he blames the voter for voting him into office as a last resort.

A19.   So when will Ghanaians stop reading politics into even how the ant walks?

A20.   Some people are relevant only when there are electoral campaigns to be wrought. Explains why in Ghana, we campaign without ceasing.

A21.   When a politician speaks, always reflect on what he is not saying. Then you will better understand what he said.

A22.   When the future you see is worse than the present, one begins to worry. And, oh, I speak of Ghanaian politicians. The tadpoles are out-jumping the toads.

A23.   They know it is easy to steal from the public purse, because the watchers are busily throwing stones at each other, in separate lines behind them, in colours matching their own, singing songs they have taught the watchers to sing - hailing them for their leadership. And, oh, the watchers are all in blindfolds. Blinded by partisanship instead of being emboldened by patriotism.

A24.   Why are politicians more concerned about what their fellow/opposing politicians think rather than what the ordinary Kojoes like you and I think?

A25.   Why are politicians at their admonishing best when in government and at their intellectual, analytical best when out of power?

A26.   Sometimes I pity the party spin doctors. Some issues just don't have a fulcrum on which a spin can be effected.

A27.   Politicians will reduce effusions with *gbeshie*-inspired confidence on political platforms if there are no cheering crowds.

A28.   I can't reconcile the pre-sentencing posturing with the post-sentencing protesting in the Montie 3 palaver. A clear mismatch in spirit and temperament. The mouth used to appeal for a loan is not the same used to repay it.

A29.   In analysing propaganda, always look out for what the person is NOT saying and what he is preventing you from saying by first saying what he says.

A30.   The NDC and NPP have opposite fortunes in terms of winning elections versus governance: weak in one aspect and great in the other, and vice versa.

A31.   The politicians are few. The followers are many. The many give the few the opportunity to play the many against one another. To maim the many. Whilst the few get another set from the many to go on a-maiming. We are the many. You and I.

A32.   You who allow your minds to be used for the price of a milk tin of gari.
No, I don't mean that semi-illiterate footsoldier only.
I refer to you who can't reason with your friend who has

another political leaning from you without throwing expletives.

I refer to you who share explosive information that you pause not to verify because it will make the other party look bad.

I refer to you who can't reason logically when your political head is gorged with hot tainted blood.

No, don't turn. I am talking to you.

A33. I learnt years ago not to use logic to understand African politics.

A34. When a politician tells me that day follows night, I still crosscheck.

A35. As the years go by and as we engage in more elections, we seem to retrogress and our conversations become more bizarre. And the electorate, you and I, seem not to get any wiser.

A36. Don't expect the politician to fight your battles for you. For the politician is the one who will ask YOU to die for HIS country. Cry your own cry.

A37. The young people in politics today, our peers, are even thinking less than our fathers whom we complain failed the nation.

A38. When a politician calls his fellow politician a thief and a liar, please pay attention. It could be the only time he is actually speaking the truth.

A39. What do the teeming semi-literate, usually unemployable and mostly irrational foot soldiers of our political parties want from their inordinate support for their parties? And from the victories of their parties? The answer to that should result in some sober reflections. That has a great impact on the quality of output from our political leadership. And on what we achieve as a nation between election campaigns.

A40. Nowhere is gullibility and lack of thinking, not to speak of critical listening, displayed than in the political arena and amidst politicos in Sikaman.

A41. When politicians challenge one another, they are on a familiar terrain. They are comfortable. They understand their language. They have a lot of rehearsed responses and a long list of dropdown excuses. They automatically go into the mode of 'You did it too; but only worse than we are doing'. The same nonsense, only managed better.

A42. A politician doesn't change his mind: he only offers fresh views based on fresh insight.

A43.   Politics is the leading cause of jaundiced minds.

A44.   Why should we invite politicians to discuss corruption? Isn't that conflict of interest?

A45.   One of the questions that has engaged my mind is the criteria by which we elect our MPs. What exactly do we expect them to do for our constituents? When we have fully analysed that question, we better assess their performance in respect of their obligations towards their constituents.

A46.   The rate at which politicians cross carpets in Nigeria, there must be a boom in the sale of vacuum cleaners.

A47.   Crisis test and reveal the character of a man. Same for governments. And ministers and officials.

A48.   How long shall they clean our coffers while we stand aside and look?

A49.   Petty rantings and effusions by ministers of state and politicians don't excite me. They make me sad. We need to elevate the standard of conversations in Sikaman.

A50.   Globally, politics is said to be a game but, frankly, in Sikaman, our politicians play too much.

A51. My strategy for receipt of governmental information: allow 24 hours for thawing, before subjecting it to analysis.

A52. Matter is neither created nor destroyed, but only moved from one state to another. So are ministers in Sikaman.

A53. Renaming. Reshuffling. Recanting. Reinstating.

A54. Consumer Alert: professionalism and politics don't mix well. Follow instructions carefully. Practitioner beware!

A55. If you want to guard your mind against deceit by politicians, increase the size of your memory bank.

A56. It is clear to me now. If you want to know the stance of a political party on an issue, take what they say when they are in power. For example, NDC on the relevance of inflation and macro-economic indicators, NPP on VAT, NDC on loans, NPP on number of ministers, NDC/NPP on planes and cars for officials, et cetera.

A57. The second term of any government is critical - it shows whether or not the first term was used judiciously. There is no longer the luxury of blaming a previous government and the mess or gains as may be derived from the first term.

A58.   As a student of society and political discourse, I find it amusing how political operatives use the same arguments on the various sides of power and use the same scripts when roles change.

A59.   We ask if the government is on track. Perhaps we need to backtrack and ask whether the government has even seen the track.

A60.   Drop the yam for what? A cocoyam? Or a cassava? The NPP will not get a victory on a silver platter and the NDC will not lose easily. Can we make a third party choice? I doubt it. Consumers are not known to transit from yam to yoghurt.

A61.   If you have patience and time, the poetic prose of politicians get revealed onto you in due time.

A62.   My new hobby is conducting content analysis of what politicians say, especially at rallies. You learn a lot about logical reasoning. Or lack of same.

A63.   Those who see everything through political lenses, keep it up. Those whose worth and relevance depends on whether or not the party you support is in or out of power, ayekoo.

A64.   When our politicians visit abroad, don't they feel ashamed when they see/experience the facilities they fail to roll out for the benefit of their citizens back home?

A65.   The party system is one of the reasons why we are where we are, the parties have become too powerful and this affects our development as a country. Our politicians, our MPs, are stooges of their parties and not true representatives of the people.

A66.   It is easy to be a politician in Ghana today – you only need to know how to apportion blame and to talk. Too much talk. We talk too much.

A67.   In election years, everyone will attempt to buy your mind for a pesewa. The response? Take every news item or post with a container of vacuum salt. Analyse. Doubt. Critique. Use your mind.

A68.   The politician likes asking questions when out of power but abhors being asked questions when in power.

A69.   The politician has a different position on the same issue depending on which side of power he stands.

SECTION B
WIT, FUN & SATIRE

B1.   Stupidity, once it overcomes its initial state of inertia, is sustained by its own momentum.

B2.   You need to know when to move before the push.

B3.   Intelligence is not measured in decibels.

B4.   The bosom of time disbosoms a tonne.

B5.   Patience and time disbosom a lot.

B6.   The beauty of spoken English is not in the accent you use, but your choice of words and sentence construction.

B7.   So fake it is not funny.

B8.   Some fit. Some are obvious. Some are out of place. Wigs.

B9.   Sustained 'shambolism' on a trajectory of steeply increasing gradient.

B10.   I watched the ant engage in a battle of wits with the camel. It was a mental bloodbath!
Unfortunately, one of them did not survive...
The camel has just been buried in the schlemiel cemetery.

B11.   It is when an umbrella is folded that you know its real dimensions.

B12. You may have truly smelt a rat, but remember also that your nose is close to your mouth.

B13. Europe is experiencing what our forefathers experienced in Africa centuries ago: migrants appearing on their shores without visas.

B14. There are many dangerous situations under the sun and one such is meeting a talkative on the way to a critical meeting at the loo.

B15. Always amazing how someone with rotten teeth can complain of getting a headache due to the stench from the passing sewage truck.

B16. You can't fake a fart.

B17. Winston Churchill said that 'success consists of going from failure to failure without loss of enthusiasm". Odekuro shows us that success consists of going from promise to promise without loss of enthusiasm.

B18. Wofa Kapokyikyi returned home that day and waited for Odekuro. He reminded Odekuro that hope, though a very good boost, does not cook yam.

B19. Gullibility combined with superstition is a very deadly mixture.

B20. A he-goat on steroids is still no match for a lion suffering a bout of malaria.

B21. The emperor is naked and the little boy to shout to bring us all to reality is naked himself. Long live the farce!

B22. Our politicians don't even know how to insult our intelligence intelligently.

B23. Whilst the masses strive to ensure their salaries make ends meet, the politicians increase their earnings to meet the ends.

B24. One of the pleasures of life is to listen to an articulate person speak nonsense with finesse and great grammar.

B25. The best way to make ends meet in Ghana is to make ends meet. Someway, somehow.

B26. Wisdom is clear in whichever language one speaks. A person who spews nonsense in English will sound the same when the message is translated into Hausa.

B27. There is no wi-fi in an African village, but you find better connection there.

B28. The best friend to have is a wise madman.

B29.   One of the pleasures of life is to observe a lady trying to hide her love for a guy.

B30.   There is nothing as dangerous as a fool who believes he is anointed.

B31.   Everyone has a naughty side.

B32.   Before you go shouting that the air is fouled, please brush your teeth first.

B33.   A woman who wants to get pregnant is the best of wives.

B34.   If you have never travelled, you insist that your chief's palace is the biggest building in the world.

B35.   Even in the land of monkeys, hw☐ n'☐ nim bi (look at his ugly face!) is used as an insult.

B36.   If we all lose our heads, who will be the heads collector?

B37.   The significance of the anus is felt when it refuses to open its mouth. No one's job is insignificant.

B38.   Appearances may be deceptive, but smell is not.

B39. The most comprehensive, reliable and accurate statistics in Ghana, which everyone agrees to and accepts and on which confident prediction, indeed regular analysis and projection are made on, is the weekly compiled records of lotto numbers.

B40. Looking at salaries in the public sector and the expenditure of most public sector workers, the gap between income and expenditure is not bridged by prayer every month.

B41. A big nose does not necessarily mean a sharper sense of smell.

B42. A well-rounded head doesn't necessarily house a well-rounded mind.

B43. He who goes round shouting that the air is fouled should not forget that the mouth is close to the nose.

B44. What God has put asunder, let no man put together.

B45. All animals are equal, but some animals have more dignity in death than when alive. Like domedo.

B46. A man thinks he chases a woman, to win her; but a careful observer of the oldest game in life knows that a man chases a woman until she catches him.

B47.   One of the key reasons why we live long in Ghana is that we have comedy all around us.

B48.   When you have your cupboard full of skeletons, you don't invite a biology teacher for furniture inspection.

B49.   Soon enough, the chicks will join the hawk in telling the hen that it is not the case that her dance is unpleasant to the eye, but that she is not even dancing at all.

B50.   In Ghana, many issues start with the vim of boiling beans and end with the dignity of a fart.

B51.   What a man says when drunk, he thought about whilst sober.

B52.   How can you ask the sparrow to lose weight?

B53.   Why seek for a level-playing field when there is no playing field?

B54.   Listen to Sikaman politicians when they call each other cheats and thieves. That is possibly the only time they speak the truth.

B55.   You know you are in Ghana when ambulances carry dead people leisurely from the hospitals whilst taxis carry sick people hurriedly to the hospitals.

B56. You know you are in Ghana when street lights are visible decorations by day and invisible shadows by night.

B57. When you have taken a generous quantity of Wofa Kapokyikyi's special and are infused with the fuse of the furious spirit, you don't go saying 'GHA-PO-HA'.

B58. I refuse to let my heart and mind go through any gymnastics with respect to the (2013) Supreme Court Election petition. I await the final verdict. Meanwhile, I smile at the false impression created by many Facebook activists who know as much about law as a waakye seller knows about the manufacturing of airplanes.

B59. This convoluted revision of tariffs is a clear case of a milk tin of gari.

B60. Height is just a number.

B61. I have good news and great news: the good news is that Odekuro says "we are not declaring load-shedding". The great news is that load-shedding will declare itself.

B62. Ah, Montie ns□ m!

B63. You have the right to keep your thoughts to yourself.

B64.   Her face reminded me of a page in my child's colouring book that has received a treatment from his box of crayons, every colour generously applied.

B65.   They asked in the village square: "Who are you to say that the fetish priest's teeth are rotten?" Only one person answered. That he can say it. My Wofa Kapokyikyi. And he says he will even go to Ok☐ mfo☐ with twapea (chewing stick) as a gift.

B66.   The beauty of patience is that, when exercised, you can live to hear the same words used yesterday to argue a position also used to debunk it tomorrow. That is why I like to watch life unfold with the attitude of Efo's favourite son, Joseph.

B67.   The beautiful thing about Sikaman is that those who know much talk little and those who talk much know little.

B68.   Ebo Nkwantabisa was known far and wide in the Assin area. A famed hunter, it was believed that if one held a finger up, Ebo could shoot it off at a hundred yards. The antelope and the duiker he had killed, the black-and-white colobus and the warthog he had subdued. He also loved to hunt another species in the land of the living: girls. And he had a similar reputation in that enterprise as well.

B69.   Even a mosquito does not get a pat on its back until it starts working hard.

B70.   There is a reason why the parrot is not considered the wisest animal in the jungle.

B71.   At birth, Kweku's father had looked intently at his son, searching for any semblance; he found one immediately – the head, and particularly the back of the head. Many had described the back of Owawani Ananse's head as resembling that of a yawning bird.

B72.   None resign, few die, none is sacked and the rest are reassigned.

B73.   It is when you are broke that you discover that you are not allergic to some food items after all.

B74.   A man who builds a house of lies usually equips it with a large window through which to escape when he gets into trouble.

B75.   That feeling you get when you discover the person who told you that drinking palmwine is a sin using akpeteshie as a mouthwash.

B76.   The days of unnerving ineptitude.

B77.   Clueless government, shambolic opposition, atrophied.

B78.   Even Roger Federer cannot respond to all the balls thrown at him.

B79.   But are we not to change the narrative? Are we only to be fed the crumbs because our ancestors have always been servants so their offspring cannot be given better food?

B80.   The most dangerous bit of all the mess we are experiencing is that we are getting used to it. When you are served effluent for long, you are not even able to distinguish it from apeprensa.

B81.   It seems that in our part of the world, in many sectors, the past looks brighter than the present.

B82.   Gbagbo baa gbo last show!

B83.   This subsidy argument by Mahama Ayariga is like stretching the description of a snake to suit a tapeworm.

B84.   Ah, what a gargantuan Ga kenkey, but it is late too. So, well …, I will let it rest in the fridge like OB overnight. Tomorrow, I will tackle it with Attamic slow-but-sureness but fortified with Amiduic kapa, together with shito as hot as Nerquaye-Tetteh. Surely, I can expect satisfaction of Woyomic proportions.

B85.	Thinking, scheming, praying, projecting, dreaming, noting.

B86.	Cynicism is not a genetic disease, it is acquired.

B87.	The billy goat that insists on being called a lion will not be the king of the jungle when transferred to the forest.

B88.	In Ghana, monkeys move by parties.

B89.	One of the most dangerous persons in the world is a retired prophet.

B90.	Even though Guinness is dark, smooth and bitter, it is not a blood tonic.

B91.	Some people do not count their chicks before they are hatched, they do better. They count them even before the eggs are laid and before determining if their chicken is a broiler or a layer.

B92.	Odekuro says because of the libation he and his chiefs have been pouring and the resulting blessings of the gods, cocoa harvest has been good and cassava tubers now look like the anantu of Yaa Konf□ . This has led to prosperity and every Kwaku, Kwekuvi and Kabutey can afford to buy an Akasanomaa radio, increasing the demand for batteries, rechargeable batteries in this case because of same prosperity to afford.

B93. Energy and power are separated or linked by the unit of time. So it has been postulated that the President separated Energy and Power to gain some time.

B94. One of the Sikaman wonders: our inability to maintain street lights.

B95. The reaction between incompetence and talkativeness in the presence of a catalyst such as an impending election results in cacophonous irritation.

B96. It is a fearful thing to be in thick Accra traffic and to have an urgent call from Nature.

B97. The similarity comes with the simplicity of the topics intertwined with the power of déjà vu: stories that remind you of your own experiences, lessons of everyday life served with a different perspective, making you look at your experiences again - resulting in new learning, all your own.

SECTION C
LOVE, FRIENDSHIPS, FAMILY & MARRIAGE

C1.   A bad marriage is like a never-healing sore; a broken relationship is a sore that got treated in time.

C2.   Don't give up your friend because of a political difference. A politician is not a better replacement.

C3.   Maintain friends that add to your life, sense and not stress.

C4.   Sometimes all our friends need is our silence. And our quiet assurance that we care.

C5.   Marry someone who will grow with you and allow you to grow.

C6.   I don't ask if I am not told, even when I can deduce. I believe with personal things when the person wants to share, he or she will. Until then, I serve friendship better by not nosing.

C7.   The respect I have for my friends dictates that there are some of them I don't discuss politics with. Politics is sometimes so emotive words are exchanged without thought and could easily mar relationships.

C8.   If you can laugh together, forgive one another and apologise to each other, you can stay together.

C9.   Marriage is best built in bytes of memories. Make it a megabyte each time.

C10.   Circumstances change and can be reversed in minutes. I advocate that couples pool resources, budget together and have an arrangement that engenders openness in financial matters. The metrics and relativities that one uses today may not be the same tomorrow.

C11.   When people marry, many stop trying. Couples in our day give up too easily, in our marriages. We are ready to fight for our jobs, for our properties, for everything else except our marriages, our relationships, our covenant with our spouses before God.

C12.   Spouses need to know that emotional love and care are as important as the physical, and not neglect each other. In the midst of work and life pressures and taking care of kids, coupled with the bluntness of affection that time, proximity and used-to-you-ness can bring to a relationship, emotional care can be relegated to the background.

C13.   The road of love is not asphalted.

C14.   One of the greatest tragedies is for marriage partners to get to the point where they just become business partners, their shares being their children and property.

C15.   The ultimate affection is when a lady allows her love to show when she should be guarded. Some men take it for granted. Wise men don't.

C16.   Marry someone whose nonsense you can tolerate.

C17.   No man is truly married until he understands every word his wife isn't saying.

C18.   If only we would treat our spouses with the same courtesy with which we handle strangers, how refreshing our homes will be!

C19.   I can never pay back my parents for their sacrifices for me. The least I can do is to care for them until their teeth fall out. In all the ways I can, I pledge to let them know that this little boy, on whose account they sold the only TV set and freezer they ever purchased in their lives, is grateful.

C20.   I don't like to romanticise role models and see them as some far-away personalities. Role models are around us all the time and the first role models children should have are their parents. Believe me, children try to become like their parents even before they understand what role models are.

C21.   In life, generally, my parents have influenced me a lot by their belief in creating a better life for me.

C22.   In love, and in the long run, nothing is as romantic as the truth.

SECTION D
GHANA & AFRICA

D1.   Our country Ghana is not big, it only has bad roads.

D2.   I stood on the map of the world and searched far and near for the nation which runs as if nothing can go wrong, never learns from its mistakes and is unprepared for any emergencies. The Spirit directed me to look under my feet.

D3.   The beautiful thing in Ghana is that we are never in short supply of excuses.

D4.   This is a nation of beautiful grammar, eloquently served by our paid public and political officials.

D5.   Over the years, our leaders took Nkrumah too serious - when he said Africans had the right to govern or misgovern ourselves - that they did both. Or rather more of the latter than the former.

D6.   Whilst other countries are flying, we are perambulating in the mud, tickling ourselves into drunken hallucination and beating our chests like the market warriors we are: luminous stones amongst rotten palm kernels.

D7.   We didn't strive to drive out our colonial masters only to have our own flesh and blood treat us like colonized people. We didn't take out foreign oppressors to replace them with indigenous ones.

D8.   The longer the title, the lesser the effort put in to work and justify that title. Africans should go easy on accumulation of titles and let our works and actions immortalise us. As the former MD of Barclays Ghana, Ben Dabrah, said in an interview, being appointed or elected into a position should not make one a hero; it is what you achieve in that position that should matter.

D9.   Sometimes upon reflecting on Ghana, the past seems brighter than the future.

D10.   I learnt something from Patrick Awuah when I listened to him once at Ato Ulzen-Appiah-inspired Bar Camp Accra. He said, at Ashesi, they don't say what they are going to do, they announce what they have done. That sank into me. In Ghana, we usually announce what we want to do even before we have tested its sustenance.

D11.   Our generation is the game-changing generation for our country and continent. We cannot join in the chant of our predecessors; we cannot think at the same level, we cannot go at the same pace. We are the generation with the greatest exposure to what better conditions can be like – let's replicate it here. We know what a country that takes action looks like – let's cut the long talk. We know not just the potential, but the actual position this nation can spring to – let's get working.

D12.   Ghana is not broke. We only have broken systems.

D13.   Ghana must work again. And the beginning of the reverse from the decline will start the day we speak Ghana and nothing else.

D14.   Ghana is not broken. It only has a citizenship who are broken into pieces and not united. Who are chained not to each other, but to parties that are not chained to the destiny of Ghana.

D15.   Ghana is not broke; it has only been broken by some greedy brethren. And the breaking train continues, unbroken.

D16.   Chatting with a friend about African currencies and the effects of speculation, I stated: vultures don't gather around healthy animals.

D17.   Nkrumah said we face neither east nor west but forward. Where are we faced now?

D18.   Nkrumah said there was a new African ready to control his own affairs. Isn't that African old now? Has s/he remained relevant to the times?

D19.   Nkrumah advised we act as men of thought and think as men of action. So why do we have so many acting only as wo(men) of superficial thinking?

D20.   An observer of sikamanosyncracies never experiences a dull day. The din of our issues reach a crescendo with the speed of a DC-10 and just like the fate of that aeroplane's name, that din tapers into the sea of forgetfulness.

D21.   Africans: one people separated artificially by borders that trace crooked lines drawn on a piece of paper somewhere in a cold land.

D22.   Nkrumah declared that we faced neither east nor west but we faced forward. But, see, we can face forward and just look at the horizon. Sometimes, as I think of Ghana, I am tempted to believe that we kept looking East and West and never made up our minds, so we just stood still.

D23.   In Africa, we are more likely to unite around a foreign/imported idea than an idea from one of us. For instance, in Ghana, we would rather adopt English or Swahili as a national language than to adopt Ewe or Ga.

D24.   Come to Africa and help! Wherever you may be in the world, there is something you can give back to the continent that gave you a name and an identity, at least.

D25.   When you have a leaking container, pouring water into it even at a faster rate doesn't keep the water level up. Oh, I Speak of Ghana.

D26.   This stupidity of sounding a siren and speeding through traffic with a coffin must be an African speciality.

D27.   We are a people steeped in gullibility combined with superstition, a very deadly mixture. If that gullibility is superintended by a group of leaders who take no action to either increase literary or even use their own literacy to improve the lot of their people, then what you get is a society which is either jogging at one spot whilst the rest of the world moves on, or doing the cha-cha-cha dance, which has become the national dance of many an African country – one step forward, two steps back.

D28.   In the past, Europe came down to Africa to traffic in humans. Today, the humans traffic themselves into Europe.

D29.   Ghanaians will rant, wind down and move on. We are adept at adapting. We are magicians. We survive. How we do it, we don't know. There will be an evening, and another day. Life goes on. C'est la vie.

D30. The annoying moment when you are really enjoying a Ghanaian or Nigerian movie which has built up a good riddle to be resolved...and then a juju man scene is introduced to solve the issue. A film reflects a society. Are we saying that is how we resolve most of our problems?

D31. Sometimes, I want to sit back, take a simplistic view and laugh at the stress of the officials at Lampedusa as they try to stop African immigrants from crossing from Libya to Europe via Italy. Did our ancestors not wake up one day to find European immigrants on our shores?

D32. As a young African who has his continent and country at heart, who is guided by the Latin expression, Pro Patria, the motto of my secondary school, Ghana National College, for the sake of the fatherland, who is of the strong view that we are the ones to build our homeland, with our sweat, blood and hands, nothing makes me angry more than to see the slow pace of development in Ghana. And to see that whilst we go so slow, our leaders who should know better continue to pat their backs and sing their own praises. For someone who has spent a year abroad and seen what a thinking and forward people can achieve, bit by bit, day by day, I get annoyed when it seems that here in Ghana, the past seems rather brighter than the future.

D33.   I would define 'Pan-Africanism' as the belief in Africa and the fact that Africa can be better. As I advocate strongly in my book I Speak of Ghana, it is up to you and I, our generation.

D34.   My cardinal belief is that the natives of the land till the land best, with passion and meaning. The advanced nations of this world built their countries by the sweat of their indigenes.

D35.   Africa's problems have been with leadership and the attitudes and actions of leaders being at variance with the reality of the problems they need to solve.

D36.   Welcome to Ghana, where we sweat the petty stuff and ignore the important matters.

D37.   The tensions in South Africa should ease! The past should not be revisited in a reverse mode, the killing of blacks was bad and the killing of white is bad as well. A human being is just that - irrespective of colour, race or form.

D38.   One of the major problems we have in Ghana is the "had I/we/he or what if" syndrome. That is why we continue to debate and berate what happened and the actors of 50 years ago. Even God cannot change the past, he can only forgive it. What are we doing today for tomorrow?

D39.   Ghana is ours. Our turn to make it rock. For good!

D40.   You know you are in Ghana when emergency shelters promised after an emergency are not built two weeks after the emergency.

D41.   Ghana is not poor; it just has porous pockets.

D42.   We have a beautiful country but we should cut the talking and start building.

D43.   The time comes when you can no longer blame your father for your woes or state of affairs. Same happens with governments.

D44.   We berate the whites for slavery and argue that the slave trade took away all our energetic and productive young men and women. Are we not practising voluntary trade today?

D45.   Our national issues are not renewed every year. They are always familiar.

D46.   Ghana@60 is a poor old man, still living in his parents' house, with a rich boy's appetite.

D47. Haven't we honoured Nkrumah enough? One day his ghost will come back and lash us for not being the new Africans he boasted about and for using his name in vain without using any of his wisdom.

D48. The Tema Motorway epitomises for me in many ways how Ghana has been managed since independence and its current state and how we have not kept with the times. Each time you dodge a pothole with the metal grills baring their teeth on the motorway, think about Ghana.

D49. Hope is a good breakfast but a bad dinner, it has been said, but in Ghana, we have deteriorated to the point of having hope for dessert after dinner.

D50. In Ghana, promises and deadlines are mounted on wheels.

SECTION E
BOOKS, LEARNING
& READING

E1. Don't just ask your kids to read. Get caught reading too.

E2. Knowledge is free at the library. Just bring your container.

E3. We go to school to learn how to learn. If all you learnt in school is the 'what' you learn and you do not leave with a desire for continuous learning, then you didn't learn at all and your learning ended when you left school.

E4. What distinguishes us from our classmates is the learning we do after school.

E5. Expand your space for knowledge storage and fill it up.

E6. Your learning ceases the moment you stop asking why.

E7. We should learn as a people to pay good money for the food that feeds the soul and mind, same as we do for the food that feeds the body.

E8. A bestseller is made one sale at a time.

E9. If six months from today, all you know is what you know today, you are archaic by more than six months. If you stop adding knowledge, you are old, irrespective of your age.

E10.   Are you practising continuous learning? Learning never ends. We are in the era of self-tuition. 'He who lives by the sea should not wash his hands with spittle.' (Nigerian proverb). Continuous learning will make you a more informed person. Continuous learning will improve your marketability. Continuous learning will guarantee that six months from now, you will not be an ignoramus.

E11.   The baby is not afraid that someone will say he/she is taking baby steps and not walking in the right way. The baby is not bothered. Don't wait to become an expert before you attempt converting your thought into action.

E12.   These days, many gadgets compete for our attention and if you sat in trotro from Odorkor to Circle, most of the passengers would be browsing on their phones rather than reading a book. Progressively, also, we have people gravitating towards more succinct and shorter text to read, and this affects our reading abilities.

E13.   Nothing can replace a good book - nothing! Unfortunately, this discipline of reading is dying in these times. We just don't read anymore. We don't study anymore. We are not adding knowledge, at all!

E14.   We are living in an era where everyone seems to have the urge, appetite and desire for fast things! Reading and appreciating what we read is fast becoming a practice of the past. And it is worrying.

E15.   In this age of knowledge, it is a sin to be ignorant or to stay ignorant.

E16.   A society that does not promote writing, documentation of its history, events and thoughts, will always have to re-invent the wheel.

E17.   It is common to think of learning as something that takes place in school, but much of human learning occurs outside the classroom and people continue to learn throughout their lives.

E18.   The best and longest lasting school is the school of life, the self-tuition school.

E19.   Continuous learning is a habit I work at honing each day. In this era of information explosion, it is a real tragedy if the Scripture quote '...my people perish for lack of knowledge' should apply to anyone.

E20.   Read critically, think critically and speak out of the depths of your learning and thoughts.

E21.   Get our kids exposed to books. Let them love books right from infancy.

SECTION F
NATION BUILDING

F1.   We need middle-ground thinkers and long-term planners in our body politic. This parochial, myopic and compartmentalised mode of Sikaman politics will take us in only one direction: backwards.

F2.   The problem in Sikaman is that we spend too much energy to plan to (and actually) announce what we intend to do that we have no energy left to actually do what we intended to do.

F3.   Is the speed at which we are moving good enough for my comfort and aspirations for this nation? Can I take a risk with audacity for four years and if it does not work out, use my manicured thumb to effect change again? Or I will continue to perambulate the well-trodden paths? That is the choice engaging my mind.

F4.   On the matter of returning home to build our nation, "home" doesn't mean one's country alone but the entire continent of Africa. There is much to do and so much we can give back. We have the land to till. And the natives till it best.

F5.   The most effective health policy and care in Ghana is the Grace of God.

F6.   On my friends' list, I have pals who have declared openly for various parties. Also, there are those who haven't declared. We debate issues, we disagree sometimes and other times we agree. What is constant is that we all love Ghana. None of us was born into a political party or has such captured on our birth certificate. What binds us is the fact that we are Ghanaians. I have seen people cross carpet and become passionate in defence of a party they lambasted in the past. That is all part of life. Parties get dissolved or go on leave. Ghana, our beloved country, remains. This election shall come to pass. But let not the ties that bind us break in the process. One Ghana! Peace to you and yours! Oseee Ghana!

F7.   I looked and saw the nonsense under the Sikaman sun; I saw the little men of the land suffer much for siphoning little and the big men of the land suffer little for siphoning much. I considered it and understood the principle at play: drink deep or pay the price.

F8.   When I reflect on the Free SHS debate, with one party saying it is possible now and the other saying, though constitutional, it is only possible in a couple of decades, I can't help but compare the tango to a similar one 55 years ago when Sikaman debated 'independence now' verses 'independence in the shortest possible' time. In my mind, not going into the merits and demerits (which I believe even the opposing camps agree on somewhat), the choice is clearly between audacity and treading slowly.

My view, then, goes beyond this topic of Free SHS. My consideration is comparing audacity and maintaining the status quo. Will I take a spring with a shot at the skies or be comfortable that what is within my grasp is good enough?

F9.   As long as our political leaders can continue to keep us crying ourselves hoarse and shouting at each other on their behalf, we will not have the time and energy to examine what they occasionally throw our way as development projects and discover that they are crumbs from the chop-table.

F10.   Council of State or Council of Elders of the ruling party in government?

F11.   The wide gulf between promise and reality in Sikaman is part of where we are and what we have become. Let's cut the talk in favour of some real progressive action.

F12.   Have our leaders collectively conspired to ensure that our past is brighter than our future?

F13.   You know you are in Ghana when you are branded 'too known' for insisting the right things must be done.

F14.   We put a freeze on recruitment of real people and recruit ghosts.

F15.   In a country where "provisional" lasted for eleven years, the word "temporary" would definitely have staying power!

F16.   It is a serious matter when our government officials keep referring us to six years ago when we ask for answers to today's problems. It is a crisis situation when they can even afford to mock their predecessors at the same time. It is an emergency when they can still manage to giggle.

F17.   Ghana must work again. And the beginning of the reverse from the decline will start the day we speak Ghana and nothing else.

F18.   When our Presidents, both ancient and modern, return from trips abroad, arriving before 5 p.m. and find a teeming crowd at the airport to meet them, does it occur to them that most of the persons in the crowd should rather be at work?

F19.   We should work together so that we will not only recall the 'good old days', but admit how we have added to those days and turn the verdict in favour of the future: so our children and subsequent generations can look to a brighter future, rather than a brighter past.

F20.   The role that public procurement plays in the rape of our nation's resources is like the elephant in the room: we all see it, but fail to talk about it. A friend once said that when public servants and politicians are excited about a project, one just needs to scratch the surface to realise that what really tickles them is the procurement bit. And the 10%. Only the dumb politician or public official steals all the funds for a project. The smarter ones skim off the project and yet deliver it.

F21.   The passion we express on radio everyday should be transformed into righteous anger at how slow we are developing this nation.

F22.   What this nation needs is a revolutionary departure from the mental contraption that politics has turned most of us into, which makes us see everything in myopic, partisan colours. We should stop the delusion that we are doing well, when in reality we are like market warriors, brave men among children. The advancement we crave as a nation, a people, a continent, will not come with this mediocrity of expectation, when peanuts are dropped onto our developmental plate in between elections, and grandiose plans are shared with us during campaigns and elections. And this goes beyond the politicians. Ordinary Ghanaians, you and I, civil servants, public workers, industry hands, managers – we all have to decide that we will put our shoulders to the wheel to drive Ghana

Incorporated forward. We cannot go forward otherwise, and we will stay stunted if we maintain the status quo.

F23.   One of the sad quiet developments in Sikaman is how steadily empty barrels are making noise to the top.

F24.   Whilst the West is looking to pump more money into drug research, we, in Ghana, are fighting with lecturers about research allowance.

F25.   Not all of us can and should enter the partisan arena. Some must stay back as umpires. Some must stay back as critics. Some must stay back as reporters. And some will be spectators.

F26.   The public sector is the engine of growth of an economy, not the private sector. No private sector drive can succeed on a foundation of a weak and retrogressive public sector.

F27.   In Sikaman, we have hundred great ideas, but implement only one. Badly. And set up a committee to investigate that one.

F28.   One of the major problems we have in our political arena and public discourse is the army of party communicators who hop from station to station spreading recycled nonsense evenly like expired margarine on a hot slice of

Nsawam bread and serving it daily to an eager populace which doesn't pause to wonder about the rancid taste of the bread and margarine.

F29. "We are on track, everything is on course" is a dangerous response to a query on how a project or plan is progressing.

F30. Are we really ready to hear views without forming opinions about people? I write to reach a wide spectrum of people. Will my political views alienate many who are here or bring more here? Can my friends here see my views either for or against the government or opposition as views of an independent-minded person?

F31. Our elders say 'akyea nso □ nbu y□' (it is bent but not broken). Nanso □ kyea pii a, □ nya akyakya, □ ntene - if it bends too much, it becomes crooked permanently (like a hunchback) and cannot be reformed/straightened.

F32. We cannot build on broken foundations. We cannot thrive on broken promises. We cannot go forth on principles which are broke, broken and breaking.

F33. Economics doesn't sleep with emotions.

F34. Economies don't respond to motivational talks.

F35.   Which is more important to teach our young ones: patriotism or politics?

F36.   We don't have a plan for anything. Whatever is not systematically structured crumbles.

F37.   We may sit and dilly-dally and continue to use hope as a strategy, only to look back to today and regret that we were not serious enough in our planning. It is said that hope is a good breakfast but a bad supper.

F38.   My first lesson in my Chemical Engineering course was the mass balance equation:

Accumulation = Input - Output

Once Output is not controlled and, is more than Input, there will be no or negative accumulation, which destabilizes the equilibrium of any system.

No matter what we tax - condoms, generators, incomes, talk, no matter where we beg from, no matter how much we get from inflows and our resources, if we do not control output and plain haemorrhage out of the system, we will have nothing as a nation to develop, to pay debts, to pay contractors, to build.

F39.   A nation that desists from thinking is never far from sinking.

F40.   So why are we so gullible? Why do we not use our minds? Why don't we pause to question? Why are we not critical? Why are we so easily deceived? Why are we like that?

F41.   Unless we all speak about our speedy spiral into the valley of national ineptitude, no-development and directionless-ness without fear of being branded, there will be no hope of a turnaround.

F42.   Urgently needed: Citizens who think, talk and behave with Ghana in mind and not their political parties.

F43.   We are not a thorough people. We don't follow through to completion.

F44.   In my work as a manufacturing/quality assurance professional, when my customers or consumers complain about a product, I give them the benefit of the doubt, listen and take time to investigate the veracity of their claims. That is not the time to drum into their heads that my product is the best and that they haven't seen the like of it before. Kumasi on my mind.

F45.   I get worried about our propensity to attack personalities rather than what they say. We should allow room for diverse opinions, and we should remember that even a faulty clock is right twice in the day.

F46.   Collectively, as a people, we have to upgrade our standards and expectations of our political leaders and ourselves, hold them and ourselves accountable for the promises they make and insist on specifics – projects, deadlines, processes, funds to be committed, and follow up! Otherwise, we will continue to be dribbled and deceived and nothing will get done.

F47.   I have decided, with the right application of respect, decorum and etiquette, to de-scorch my words and share my views. I will no longer stay in the camp of foolish advisors who insist that the Omanhene is wearing expensive kente when all he has on is a band of dirty see-through lace.

F48.   When an issue breaks, I usually prefer that the opposition doesn't pick it as an issue and run with it on behalf of citizens. Because once it becomes an issue between politicians, it becomes a game of football, a friendly match between politicians who are opponents in public and friends in private. The issue takes the form of the ball to be kicked about only on the field of play without any intention of scoring goals that count to the benefit of the citizens.

F49.   When citizens, ordinary citizens challenge politicians; when they challenge their governments on issues, the politicians become uncomfortable. They don't know how to fight citizens who act only in their individual and national interests.

F50.   Changing Africa, one mind at a time.

F51.   It has been said that in a typical African country with two PhD holders, one is the President and the other is in exile! That aberration must stop. We must demonstrate that the land is big enough to accommodate more than one wise person. We need all hands, heads and hearts on deck, dedicated and focused on the renaissance of Africa and its development.

F52.   Happy Republic Day! May we use the day to think. About Ghana. About lost opportunities. About A Better Ghana that actually Moves Forward, not as the politicians promise to deliver, but as we citizens endeavour to create.

F53.   When you are in government, a position of public trust or authority, the difference between a gift and a bribe is almost non-existent.

F54.   We are a nation of beautiful intentions.

F55.   Our problem in Ghana is not the lack of ideas. Neither is it not knowing what to do. Our biggest problem is lack of excellent execution.

F56.   This silly strategy of political parties comparing who made a bad move in a better way, this attitude of 'X also did it, why didn't you complain then?' must stop if we are to make any headway in our development in this beautiful nation of ours.

F57.   How can Africa improve if we don't want to stay, sweat and swim against the tide of under-development and turn our economies around? Who is to give the hope back? Who is to change the language we use? Who is to enervate us, inspire us, bring us the va-va-voom? It will not be the politicians, I can guarantee you. It will be us, the ordinary citizens.

F58.   As the nation seeks to plug holes in its burgeoning expenditure, procurement is a low hanging fruit.

F59.   What this nation needs is a revolutionary departure from the mental contraption that politics has turned most of us into, which makes us see everything in myopic, partisan colours. We should stop the delusion that we are doing well, when in reality we are like market warriors -

brave men among children. The advancement we crave as a nation will not come with this mediocrity of expectation, when peanuts are dropped into our development kitty in between elections, and grandiose plans are shared with us only during campaigns and elections.

F60.   For NGOs, check where the bulk of their funds is spent on and you will understand why most of them have no impact. Development aid can only be an aid, development must come from the communities and support should ultimately help to make the communities self-supporting, for them to own their own development agenda. Ask yourself why the northern part of Ghana has the highest number of NGOs and yet is so underdeveloped. By the way, that is a microcosm of what Africa is.

F61.   Politics is to help the country transform, progressively. I believe in baby steps, in a nation making progress daily. Our politics today is full of noise, not vision and planning. Our politicians have taken over even the institutions that should outlive their 4-year cycles, institutions that should be apolitical and help us plan decades ahead. So what we have is a 4 year cycle that is full of campaigning for a good two years and we are left with only two years of work, based on at most a four-year development plan. I ask: who is thinking for Ghana?

Who is planning for Ghana? Do you know the agenda for Ghana for 2054? At best, it sits in a manifesto that has no broad-based input and support.

F62. Too many thoughts as I go through the gates of my mind. Resisting the urge for comparison. But then, again reflecting on the poem I have been musing over for the past few weeks, titled 'Why I Gripe'. When I gripe about my land, it is not because we haven't come any further than when we started off, but because we could have gone much further. When I gripe, it is not because I don't see that we are better than most of our neighbours, but because today, when you talk about neighbours, it is not geographical neighbours, but global neighbours without borders. When I gripe, it is not for the fact that we are better than the worst, but because we are worse than the best. When I gripe, it is not because I am not thankful, but because I can see that what we see as the future potential is what should have been our present. When I Gripe.

F63. Fundamental to the labour agitations is a feeling of the workers' unions that the national cake is being treated with what is prevailing is what I call the Elephant Phenomenon: when some people approach the cake, the backside of the elephant is given to them - fleshy, soft, chunky and easy to cut. When others approach the cake, the elephant is turned around and the tusk is given to them - hard, brittle, bony and just impossible to cut.

F64.   My view is that we usually confine public service to
        only politics. Perhaps the dictionary definition is not on
        my side, but I see public service as being bigger than
        politics. I am more intent on being bigger than a
        politician, whom I increasingly find is parochial, at least
        in Ghana.

F65.   Our political parties don't impress me. Our democracy
        doesn't seem to bring development. Our progress and
        even the proper functioning of our governments appear
        arrested, impeded and controlled by parochial party
        interests. I fear that the parties are destroying the state.

F66.   Young men and women are causing wealth loss to their
        generation because they are sitting on inert ideas, bottled-
        up potential energy and scratching the ground when they
        should be gliding the skies and perambulating with the
        stars.

F67.   Years ago, we were talking 'Vision 2020'. 2020 will soon
        hit us and we will wonder what happened to our vision.

F68.   Who is to give the hope back? Who is to change the
        language we use? Who is to enervate us, inspire us, bring
        us the va-va-voom? It will not be the politicians, I can
        guarantee you. It will be us, the ordinary citizens.

F69.   We need both mindset and attitudinal change.

F70.   Did the culture of silence in the eighties produce citizens of silence?

F71.   Don't give up your friend because of a political difference. A politician is not a better replacement.

F72.   Is it not sad that when we reflect on our best leaders, we go back 50 years?

F73.   Shortage of ideas. Shortage of action. Shortage of decorum. Shortage of common sense. Shortage of gas. Shortage of aviation fuel. Shortages.

F74.   Just take a minute. Reflect on how you felt about the Black Stars' performance in the AFCON. Consider what you really have to say to Kwesi Appiah and his boys. Think about what you really want the GFA to do with his appointment and the changes you yearn for in the team and who you want on board. Do you have all those packaged? Good. Pause. Replace Kwesi Appiah and the Black Stars with our political leadership and their teams. Do you see what you should really be saying to and about their performance and what you want of them?

F75.   Where from this culture where we speak from our stomachs instead of from our minds? Where political patronage defines the exercise of our speech and the fear of being tagged restrains us from expressing our views on national issues?

F76.   Our problem, as a nation, is not a scarcity of resources — human, natural, or intellectual; our problem is our unwillingness or our lack of motivation to take action on what we know is right. We are good at diagnosing the root causes of problems but so pathetic at action. If we would all exhibit the world-class attitude and fighting spirit plus the urge to die for the name of our nation as the Black Stars do, what a nation we would have!

F77.   We don't plan anything and the future just seems to happen to us, without our input. All we seem to do is to just show up.

SECTION G
PROVERBS & SAYINGS

G1. She who refuses to go to the stream to fetch water should not berate the one who does and breaks the pot.

G2. The ability to carry a load is not dependent on the size of the head, but on the strength of the neck. The ability to make a good argument is not dependent on the size of the mouth, but the depth of the mind.

G3. Loss of power declutters the mind and descales the eyes.

G4. Expensive doesn't mean good quality.

G5. A bad name doesn't clear itself by entreaties.

G6. Sometimes, what you haven't said speaks volumes.

G7. I just allow time to be the judge of my thoughts and opinions.

G8. The tongue may have its say, the stomach may have its swag, but in the end, the anus must give way for the village of life to have a fine day.

G9. Bitterness has never made any person better.

G10.   There are two types of liars: good liars and bad liars. If you can't be a good liar, or if you have a bad memory to be consistent in lying, just restrict yourself to speaking the truth.

G11.   One can only say that action speaks louder than words and the real intent of an organisation can be determined by where the management puts its money and not necessarily its mouth.

G12.   The blessedness of time.

G13.   Words past answering the present. In some cases, we have words present answering and judging the past.

G14.   A big head does not necessarily contain a 'big' or sharp mind.

G15.   I learnt years ago not to argue or attempt to reason with people incapable of listening and even considering different and, sometimes, superior opinions. I learnt that persisting in my bid to change their minds drains me whilst they are rather invigorated in the juice of ignorance. There is much more to do in life than entreating a crab to act like an octopus, even though they may look alike.

G16.   When you keep water in a container for too long, it begins to smell. But you don't replace that with water which is not deodorised.

G17.   Rome was not built in a day; but it was built every day.

G18.   We know less than we think we know; we are better than we think we are.

G19.   You are responsible for how you feel and how you will behave. You should not be like a chameleon whose colour will become red-hot because the fire in the other person is burning. You decide how you behave - absolutely - not anyone else.

G20.   The worst person to have in a position of responsibility is an incompetent talkative.

G21.   Our beliefs about our abilities and the capabilities we have are usually the limiting reactants in the chain reaction of our lives.

G22.   People will doubt you, but do you doubt your own self? People will insult your integrity, but do you trust yourself? If you are at peace with yourself and with God, you can be at peace with the world.

G23. Words are cheap, but they gain greater worth when they first minister to the speaker of the same.

G24. When you go on a path you wish will take you to Brahabebome, don't think that everyone else is going there. There may be a junction ahead.

G25. Not all paths need to be trodden. Not all questions need to be answered.

G26. An idle brain is the devil's workshop.

G27. Sometimes what you haven't said speaks volumes.

G28. Wisdom does not shout.

G29. Don't envy my sunny days when you have no idea of my dark nights.

G30. A bulldog, no matter how ferocious it is, cannot be called a lion.

G31. He who has crossed an inch with distinction can cross a foot and a mile. Diligence, industry, determination, inch-by-inch, block-on-block.

G32. If you won't push someone up, the least you can do is not to pull him down.

G33.   The best capital - thoughts and ideas.

G34.   Having the courage to speak one's mind is as important as knowing when the time is right to do so.

G35.   Wisdom is not genetically-acquired.

G36.   We know less than we think we know; we are better than we think we are.

G37.   It is not in the multitude of words that wisdom is found. That's why the parrot is not considered the Sage of the Jungle.

G48.   He who speaks all he thinks, at the same time he thinks, will never be considered wise.

G39.   In giving a man his freedom, you gain his loyalty. Most of the time.

G40.   Even the ant gets to its destination as long as it doesn't stop.

G41.   Wisdom is evident in whatever language it is expressed in. I have heard some foolish stuff expressed eloquently in English and have lapped at sense spoken in Twi. So I don't get this so-called elitism because someone cannot speak English. Some of the wisest in our history have not been in classrooms and only a visit to a palace or rural gathering would confirm that.

G42.   The future is not that far.

G43.   Look around you today and you will see many people who need encouragement. Encourage someone today. You may be creating a writer of Empower Series! Indeed, we all need encouragement.

G44.   Trouble, it is said, is like a storm: it doesn't rain, it pours.

G45.   If you cannot make your point in three minutes, you haven't thought about and through it well enough.

G46.   Every idea is most vulnerable at the conception stage and no matter how big the Odum tree looks today, it was a seedling yesterday and a seed the day before.

G47.   The test of your anchor is in the storm, not at dock. The test of your faith is in times of crisis, not in peacetime.

G48.   Someone can make use of the kindness you are capable of showing.

G49.   We only get what we tolerate. And if we exhibit a craving for nkatie burger, surely we will be fed peanuts. Or even peanut-flavoured chippings.

G50.   Truth, like a calabash, will always float to the surface no matter how hard and how long you push it under water. Same goes for character.

G51.   Thinking is an exothermic activity, and should convert potential energy to kinetic energy.

G52.   Not all gifts are meant for your good. Some appointments are traps.

G53.   Good memory helps to recognise hypocrisy.

G54.   You don't need good memory if you speak the truth.

G55.   Thinkers perish; thoughts and ideas do not.

G56.   Usually, those who crave for mercy the most show mercy the least.

G57.   Many of us take off with passionate anger on the basis of one word when we haven't even finished reading the sentence.

G58. Don't ask why I am still awake. Rather, ask what is keeping me awake.

G59. A single head cannot constitute a conference.

G60. We are bigger than we think but often as small as our biggest fear.

G61. The height of your self-esteem determines the available volume for your success.

G62. The most effective emancipation comes from knowing yourself.

G63. Ignorance is a false force-multiplier.

G64. You cannot change what you tolerate.

G65. A life well lived is one that has survived through stress, triumphed through trials, and has come back after a setback. A life that is still being lived with optimism after challenges. A life well lived is not one that has not been without tsunamis.

G66. When God does it in His due time for you, He does it right.

G67. Every instance in your life is an opportunity to impact someone's life and to be impacted on as well.

G68. We have had enough motivation. What we now need is provocation.

G69. We all get ideas in the shower. Don't you? Well I do. It is the translation of ideas, the deployment of strategy into action and the movement of blueprints from the drawing board into the performance sphere that matters.

G70. Not all intelligent people talk sensibly when they have their backs against the wall.

G71. The test of the excellence of the ship's design and the captain's skills is in the midst of a storm and not when the ship is docked at the harbour.

G72. When both the lead and the leader throw up their hands in despair, then there is no hope of repair.

G73. If you worry about what people make out of everything you say, your mouth will smell out of inactivity.

G74. We need to distinguish between arrogant pride and assertiveness. One is negative and undesirable; the other is pure, spiritual and empowering.

G75.   He knows how to talk best who knows when to keep quiet.

G76.   The best time for a man to fall is the immediate moment after he has been acknowledged as a hero.

G77.   How you treat the talent you have is a reflection on how you view it in the total picture of what you are here on earth to do.

Section H

Advice and Instruction

H1.   Don't be afraid of being branded. You could be creating a new brand, charting a new course. You could be the next benchmark.

H2.   Knowing what to do and yet not doing it, procrastinating, thinking of how to do it perfectly, yet holding back and worrying about the passage of time: that will give you a headache! Take the pill of action and welcome your relief!

H3.   I once said that the beautiful thing about patience and the bosom of time is that words used to put someone in his/her place today will be the same words that embarrass or implicate the speaker tomorrow. In the matter of the current misogynistic utterances, however, the time lap is microscopic. It is, in this case interestingly, embedded in the proverb that says when you point the index finger at a person, three fingers are pointing back at you.

H4.   Don't just make money. Make an impact too.

H5.   Go over that fear of failure and try something you always feared to do. Be bold!

H6.   Don't rush through the garden of life without stopping to smell the roses.

H7.   Reflect before you reply.

H8.   Cross-check before you forward.

H9.   Think before you forward.

H10.   Pause before you post.

H11.   Pray before you proceed.

H12.   Drink deep at the feet of mentors.

H13.   Disengage from vim-diminishers and lock onto vim-givers.

H14.   It is the one who goes to the stream to fetch water whose pot can break. Don't be afraid of breaking your pot. Keep going to the stream. Keep doing you.

H15.   Speaking boldly and damning the tagging, knowing that those who damn you today may praise you tomorrow as the truth you speak tickles them with different strokes. In the end, your consistency will expose their inconsistency.

H16.   Words and the blessedness of time. Words are two-edged swords. Always season your words with Royco. And preserve them well. They may be served back to you for breakfast.

H17.   Don't go chasing after Fame; she is an evasive lady. Be diligent in the work your hands find to do, doing it to the best of your abilities and affecting lives, and Fame will find you.

H18.   Before you speak today, think. After thinking, act. As you act, check how your action today will affect tomorrow.

H19.   Don't say all you think about; think about all you say.

H20.   Learn to control your temper. Don't do anything in a rash manner. Be careful that one action in a second does not derail your life for a generation. Let your pillow be your counsellor and by all means, let it be absorbent as well.

H21.   Let's be doers. Doers make mistakes but they move and achieve.

H22.   Every instance in your life is an opportunity to impact someone's life and to be impacted on as well. No moment is insignificant. If you invest in someone's life at any moment, you have no idea what that person may turn out to be, or what your seed will turn into. A chance meeting with a fellow prisoner and interpreting his dream was all that was needed to bring Joseph's name to the attention of the Pharaoh of Egypt.

H23.   Whatever you say today, think about tomorrow.

H24.   In life, I have learnt one very important lesson which I keep: never talk when angry and not in control of my faculties. I use it also in my marriage. I see its application in politics too. Never talk just after a defeat. Or minimise the talk.

H25.   Our mental blocks are more formidable than the physical ones. Bob Marley said it when he asked us to emancipate ourselves from mental slavery. You first think what you become. The physical starts from the mental and the spiritual.

H26.   Spend quality time thinking about your future.

H27.   Don't be a slave to someone else's attitude.

H28.   People grow and change, some for the better, some for the worse. Never tag anyone as insignificant based on current circumstances.

H29.   Resolve today not to sulk and slack as you wait for due time to arrive. Be diligent. Improve yourself.

H30.   Make a plan to review what you have learnt every three months, at least. Learn by experience, observation, listening and reading. Do this continually and consistently.

H31.   When you get to the end of the rope, tie a knot and hang on. When you are tired of hanging on, pray for strength to go on. When all fails, let go and let God. He steps in when we let Him know it is beyond us.

H32.   Be controlled from the inside of you. Be controlled by your standards. Be motivated by your decisions. Have high standards of behaviour that ride over the negative noise of others. Laugh with those who laugh, mourn with those who mourn, but don't mourn when you don't want to, and laugh at those who laugh at you if you want to. Determine not to be a photo-sensor that brightens the lights only when people are nice to you.

H33.   Our past should not imprison us. Our past should only guide us. Learn from the past, deal with the lessons and move on. The future is bright, but it shines only on those who are willing to enter it with the attitude of learners and doers. You can be such a person!

H34.   Let no one despise your youth, but become an example of the believers in word, in conduct, in love, in spirit, in faith, in purity. Don't underrate the influence you can have in your youth. Don't think you have all the time to make a difference in this world. Recognize that both brown and green leaves fall to the ground.

H35.   Brown leaves fall, green leaves fall as well. Not all seedlings become big trees. What you gotta do for the world, your society, for one person, do it now, start, don't wait for an elusive tomorrow.

H36.   Your name is a brand. Build its brand equity, as a legacy for your descendants.

H37.   The ideas we have for our generation can only be remembered if they are rolled on the wheels of action. May we affect our societies for good! There is no time to waste!

H38.   Stop. Think. Act.

H39.   Beware of what you fear. Don't overestimate and empower your fear.

H40.   Life is too short to be angry. Get over it and move on. Smell the flowers.

H41.   Don't say everything you think about; think about everything you say.

H42. Don't cause wealth loss to your generation. Life is too short to be little. You have an impact to make on your generation and the time to start was yesterday. In whatever capacity you find yourself, you can make a difference.

H43. The time to build the future for our children is now, to give them a head start. If our descendants will enjoy the fruit of our labour, the time to do the planting is now.

H44. Do your thing in your corner. Do it with passion and excellence. The world will notice. Soon.

H45. Keep knocking, don't stop, don't lose hope. One day, the doors will begin to open even before you knock; grace, your name and brand will do the auto-knocking and the doors will be opened by people, to invite you in.

H46. Treat everyone you meet with their potential in mind.

H47. Do your work with a clear conscience and with professionalism. Without fear of being tagged. Those who say you are evil today because you are wearing green whilst they wear pink, will tomorrow call you friends because they will soon begin to wear green. The taggers change their tags whilst you continue in your lane.

H48.   "Don't automate what you cannot control manually." A lesson taught me by Unilever veteran margarine process engineer, Hans Bosman. He added that such a situation represented carpet over dirt. A recent event reminds me of this truism.

H49.   Prioritise the voices you will listen to, the good and the bad. Cut out the negative voices. Keep your eyes on the top of the tower.

H50.   Be less generous with your advice: live it instead. Living the example is the best advice you can ever give.

H51.   None ever made an impact by following convention. Let none define and restrict you. Fly free and chart your path.

SECTION I
SOCIAL MEDIA

I1.   When engaging on social media, always remember there are three categories of people: those who can't be educated or enlightened, those who don't wish to be enlightened, and those who have both the desire and ability to be educated. Knowing which type you are engaging with helps to be efficient in dispensing your energy.

I2.   All this reposting of Facebook guidelines and disclaimers remind me of the tale in which everyone starts running because someone said the world was coming to an end, until one stopped to ask the root cause. Always ask why.

I3.   Don't be deceived into thinking that social media is just virtual. The line that divides virtual and real world is now made of dew.

I4.   There are a number of personalities on social media that I may never have had the opportunity to read and learn from, but for this technology. I follow them and read almost everything they post. They attract their kind to their posts and pages. I read and learn. I visit their pages mostly to observe and learn, and mostly on the quiet. I am grateful for the library of knowledge that this platform offers.

15. Social media. Such a revealing platform. Where one's intelligence is revealed. And the opposite too.

16. Seriously, perusing the timelines of political operatives in Sikaman scares me. Forget grammar and syntax. The values, thoughts and opinions are sometimes frightening. Frightening still is the realisation that these folks fear not to take positions and responsibilities that those who consider themselves more qualified hesitate to touch even with long poles.

17. Social media has helped make the world flatter and reduced the degrees of separation, leading to the situation where many can interact with people who, but for this platform, may never have had the privilege to meet or speak with. That is the opportunity social media brings. But it does come with responsibilities. Not to take this opportunity for granted and not to throw decorum to the dogs. The line between virtual and real life is getting thinner and is lately made of morning dew. Manners matter on social media.

18. Social media has made gossiping so easy.

19. What is a gossip's best attribute? I will tell you: The ability to propagate and spread information he or she hasn't even verified.

I10.   The benefits you derive from FB and Twitter depends largely on what appears in your newsfeed and timeline.

111.   We lament about the politics of insults engulfing our discourse and yet we dabble in it in our small ways on our walls. We are the change we seek. Only those who have either lost or actually lack (in the first place) the ability to debate intellectually resort to insults. I don't and won't insult. And in the same vein won't allow myself to be subjected to that treatment. Not here. Not on your wall. I don't need the stress.

SECTION J
LIFE & CAREER

J1.   If you can still feel shame, you should thank God for that. It means you still have hope of recovery. If you cannot feel shame...

J2.   Sometimes one is a very good backing vocalist, but not a good lead vocalist.

J3.   I have enough experience in my short life to know that life is too short to go through with a short wall of tolerance.

J4.   There is a phenomenon known as "being promoted to your level of incompetence".

J5.   Change begins with a question.

J6.   I started living the day I finally accepted the fact that I couldn't like everyone and that not everyone will like me.

J7.   Success in life is not just about the destination, but the journey itself. Make time to smell the roses, make friends, create memories, and enjoy the moments.

J8.   Most of my mates who have gone on to make great strides in their careers didn't make even second class. Funny I was counselling someone just last week with this point. It happens that those who make lower than first class have more holistic approaches to university life and make the most of it beyond just academics. These life skills tend to serve them well after exiting the classroom. And, oh, I say this as one who obtained a first class, but also happens to be a student of life.

J9.   The strength of your walk is not in the loudness of your voice, but the hearts your voice can reach. The strength of your faith is not in the volume of your words, but what your words are able to accomplish.

J10.   It has been said that a picture is worth a thousand words. But sometimes, a picture is not enough to capture the entirety of the experience - the smells, the feeling, the cool, the heat, the pulsations...many times during the drive between the north and the south of Ghana, I stopped, picked the camera and tried to capture the moment or the view. On many occasions, I just paused and sat back in the car - the picture didn't, couldn't do justice.

J11.   The greener pasture on the other side could be a collection of artificial grass.

J12.   What was the tallest mountain in the world before Everest was discovered? Answer: Everest. The fact that we didn't know Everest existed didn't mean it was shorter. It still was waiting to be discovered. Same with your potential.

J13.   Think about five, ten, twenty years from now. Reflect on what you are doing today. Will you be proud of it down the ages?

J14.   Life is not a buffet - where you pick all the choice bits. It's table d'hôte. The meal comes and you may love the protein, but not the carbs.

J15.   Time heals; time cools. Time changes our outlook, perceptions and views. Our pillows can absorb wrath. Our pillows can give us counsel in difficult times.

J16.   We all need care. Usually, those with the seemingly tough exteriors have the softest and most delicate interiors. And that goes for both sexes.

J17.   Many of us are reactive, not proactive. We react. We hit back. We are 'an eye for an eye' practitioners. We attack when we are attacked, with good measure. Our barometer reads from the environment and makes us act accordingly. We are mirrors that reflect the anger in others, the bad attitude in the other person, the negative comments of others. Let me show you a higher level of living.

J18.   My view of life is that I am a sum total of all the experiences I have had, both pleasant and unpleasant. So, no, I don't have regrets.

J19.   When you have defined yourself, circumstances don't define you – they only refine you.

J20.   Failure is a part and fact of life even for successful people. The key is: what are you going to do with and about failure? The answer to that, matters.

J21.   Many people who blow hot air and exhibit perpetual pomposity have not been taught by life. I always look at them with the expression of a pensive cat.

J22.   In your planning, plan as if you are going to live forever; in your living, live as if you are going to die today. Prepare for tomorrow, but affect a life today. You may not have the luxury of time to do all you want to do tomorrow.

J23.   My lesson from Asamoah Gyan's progress: never listen to naysayers, including your own doubts. The journey from reject to elect is powered by belief, persistence and hardwork.

J24.   You don't need to be great to touch a life, but keep on touching lives and you will be great.

J25.   There is more to life than what you are seeing today.

J26.   I refuse to just exist; I want each day, each moment, to be meaningful. And I want to be relevant, at least to one person.

J27.   Don't settle for shyness. Don't teach your kids to be shy. If you haven't started the journey away from the Shy City, you'd better start now. A second more may be too late.

J28.   The problem with most of us is that we don't spend good and quality time in the learning phase and rush on to the next, half-baked. The quality of the performance one has on the big stages of life is usually determined by the quality and quantity of preparation time spent off stage.

J29.   The past can only be a pointer to the future. Your past is not as important as what you do with it, and how you move on to seize the future. Your past may define your present, but it shouldn't define your future. Your past may colour your future, but it shouldn't limit what you can become. Your past may be the starting point, but it surely cannot determine the extent to which you can go. You may start from a pit, but can end up in Pharaoh's Palace.

J30.   I learnt very early in my career that effort is not rewarded; only results.

J31.   Life is a business to be worked at and lived, not just
        dreamed about, and that in doing this, we need to be
        'learning people' – there is an example, a message, a
        lesson, a warning or a moral you can discover in every
        scene of the play called 'life.'

SECTION K

GOD & RELIGION

K1. Before you go out there trusting the prophet, can you please spend a few minutes checking with the Lord whether the prophet is still in active service?

K2. As we move into the campaign period, the false prophets will also move into their peak season: claiming to speak for God and yet predicting victory for opposition candidates, as if God swings a pendulum to make His mind and casts lots of different days with different outcomes. And when their predictions swing, they won't come back to apologise that they didn't speak with God before speaking to us on His behalf.

K3. The arrogance and shallowness of the modern day charismatic. We have a lot to learn from the spiritual men of old as well as the Billy Grahams of our time. Noise, sweat, heat and passion do not make us deep. Our faith is turning into divination and soothsaying. God help us repent!

K4. We have turned the worship of God into divination. The reason why we don't have those "magicians" and money-doublers we experienced during my growing up days in the 80s and 90s is that many of them now perform from pulpits and broadcast from radio and TV stations, in the name of the Lord.

K5.   No man is an atheist. The fact that you don't believe in God is a belief in itself. I chose to believe in God. In Him, I have found my Saviour.

K6.   I am not nervous about what lies ahead. I am quite reflective and thoughtful about what I intend to do, and I believe in a God who holds my future as well and directs my steps.

K7.   What some of our pastors are peddling in the name of Christianity, and what some congregations are accepting, is appalling. We need to reinforce that we all have direct access to the Lord, right to the throne room. The fast-food mentality should stop; we should teach the virtue of working for our possessions, making time to search the scriptures, praying and pouring ourselves in prayers and supplication.

K8.   Bliss, perfect bliss, when we abide in Him who can bless! In Him!

K9.   The privilege to tell you my need, With knowledge you'll pay heed;
        The Holy Spirit you then give as a seal, Even to increase my zeal;
        Your Word you give, My sins you forgive;
        Light to guide my way,

As I step through the day;
Oh I love to talk to you,
When the leaves still hold dew.

K10.   Be careful when people make you feel like a saint when you are only a sinner saved by grace.

K11.   The snuff of faith I sniff each day is enough to fuel every facet of my life.

K12.   There are many people parading themselves as men of God just because they quote the Bible. Christianity, for me, is more than a religion. It is an experience. It is a personal relationship that should affect the character of the person and how connected the person is to God, should show in his deeds. The Bible talks about fruits defining the tree and same applies.

K13.   We step into the unknown each day, and we have no idea what that day holds. But God knows, because He is the architect and creator of the future. If we will only hold onto His hands and step out with Him, we can have no fear of tomorrow.

K14.   Are Christians in Ghana brought up narrow in what we read and are exposed to? There were topics and areas we were asked not to explore. I tell people that I am a writer who is a Christian rather than a Christian writer - there is a difference for me. For the former, it means I am not limited in what I write about, but certainly consider issues against my upbringing. Should we not have exposure and then build on the capacity for discretion and making good choices? Shouldn't same be applied to how we bring up our children?

K15. What God does for another is ample testimony that He has the capacity, capability and desire to meet my own needs.

K16. In Scripture, prophets also acted as counsellors to kings. Today's pastors and prophets should learn to distinguish between prophecy and counsel.

K17. Sometimes, chrife people (Christians), as we know them, are the most un-Christlike of all people.

SECTION L
PASSION & DREAMS

L1.   In the work of a genius, we recognise our own unexpressed and dormant thoughts.

L2.   Nobody knows your dreams like you do.

L3.   The educated African is the most afraid to take risks on his dreams.

L4.   Sometimes you have to converse only with yourself to be able to hear your thoughts.

L5.   Many of us don't dream; more dangerously, many of us don't spend quality time thinking. We worry, yes, but we do not think. We don't project ourselves into the future. We don't utilize imagination. For many who do dream, what is lacking is the translation of the dream into reality and the tenacity to hold on to the dream when the going gets tough.

L6.   Dreams are very powerful because they energise and embolden us. You can change your stars if you want to! And you can do that by your dream and by pursuing them. When you have a dream, you have something to live for.

L7.   The law of inertia makes us hesitate to move with our ideas and dreams most times; but as with the strength of momentum, once we overcome inertia and put in effort, the initial effort is able to turn the wheel such that the momentum from the wheel is enough to accelerate our improvement and success.

L8.   If you don't attempt something you haven't done before, how can you learn? If you don't tackle a new challenge, how can you grow? If you don't stretch your limitations, how can you reach beyond the skies?

L9.   You won't make a difference by doing what everyone else is doing. Don't be afraid to be different.

Section M
Writing

M1.   Tip for writers: do not use idioms, similes and such expressions that even J. H. Mensah and K. B. Asante have stopped using.

M2.   Tip for writers: Read.

M3.   Years ago, I learnt about the power of word-pictures, defined as "phrases we read or write that we can SEE even WITHOUT ILLUSTRATIONS". They are so vivid. Learn them and use them.

M4.   We are seeing a rejuvenated interest in writing in Ghana, but are constrained by the dearth of publishing opportunities.

M5.   I prefer to refer to my book as reflective, rather than motivation. The analogy in the differentiation is this: a motivational book may provoke you, positively, to start running, in whatever direction - that is speed. A reflective book, which is more than yet inclusive of motivational, will cause you to run, in a direction, knowing where and why you are running – that is velocity. Because it matters not how hard you row the boat if you are headed in the wrong direction.

M6.   Through my writings, my earnest hope is that I may be able to change even one mind. If I can change one such mind, I would have contributed to the agenda of building our nation, our continent, our world.

M7.   I look at my writing as more than a hobby, I see it as a ministry, as the main vehicle and medium for me to impact my generation and beyond. I view it as my ministry and a legacy I can leave.

M8.   For writers, I wish to encourage us to document our thoughts as Africans. We erroneously say that Africans don't like reading, but my humble submission is that we need more literature relevant to us as well, and therein lies my passion to see more African writers come after the generation of the Achebes, Sutherlands, Soyinkas and Ata Aidoos. We need more African writers, writing our own African stories, for our African readers.

M9.   As an engineer/author, I seek to be an example to our youth. That they can experiment and explore, and not to let their scope and influence on their generation be restricted by their formal training, to stop restricting themselves to the box or pigeon-hole when they can go beyond the perimeter and reach the pinnacle of their potential. To grasp the verity that talents cannot be tamed and should be employed for the universal good of mankind. With these scripts, I attempt to instigate thought, provoke reflections and educe action.

M10. This is what I aim to achieve with my writing - for my readers to pause, think and act.

M11. I have been working at honing my online marketing skills since 2008. I look at it with a long term view: not just marketing books, but creating an online brand name, which hopefully should translate into offline recognition. So I use all the outlets: Facebook, Twitter, emails and via my website. In between the release of my books, I ensure that two things are happening: writing and sharing articles, stories and anecdotes plus one liners as well as interacting with my readers.

M12. I see writing as therapy. When I write, it is like transferring the pain from my heart to the paper and when I do encounter similar situations again, I go back to read and minister to myself. I can say that I take the prescription, 'Physician, heal thyself', very seriously.

M13. Story telling is natural to most Africans and even when we sat by the fireside to listen to our parents, a lesson was delivered in the form of a story.

M14. My very first article, published in Through the Gates of Thought, was written in 1993 - so I trace my writing life to that year. I was 18 years old then. But my appreciation of the literary form and my involvement in things literary actually started much earlier, in preparatory school, in the early 1980s when each class had to perform a play a day before the vacation day ... Small beginnings, appreciation of the arts, learning the rudiments of prose and poetry.

M15.   Writing – I create. Music – I consume.

M16.   We practise oral tradition in most African cultures, where the thoughts, ideals and knowledge of the family, tribe or clan are transmitted from one generation to the other without a writing system. However, this system is flawed in the sense that a lot of African innovation, experience and culture have been lost.

M17.   I think of my descendants ... two, three or four generations from now; I think of my children...forty, fifty years from now; I try to remember the stories my dad shared with me about his life experiences. Will my descendants know what I am going through today, what my wishes were for my generation and for them? Can the lessons I have picked up from the varied peregrinations in my life be crystallised for eternity, for the benefit of those yet unborn?

M18.   I write about everyday events, common thoughts, normal issues - but in a style that distils the key essence of life's lessons.

M19.   The stories will cause you to pause and think, think and reflect, reflect and take action - an action for a positive change. Through these, I seek to affect my society, community, continent, world - one mind at a time.

M20.   I write in chunks - a chapter at a time. For my books, I circulate the articles, chapter by chapter first and get more inputs/feedback from my online readers and friends, to help enhance the final product.

M21.   I never send out the first draft - one rule of mine is to let the sun go down on my writing.

M22.   Usually, I would have the idea in my mind, and would ruminate on it for some time. It took me three years to write one particular article; some articles take me a week from inception to finish.

M23.   My principle is to write, think about my ideas or read daily. At least two hours a day. When I write, it is usually at dawn: when the world is asleep, my thoughts are clearer.

M24.   Seeing my writing as an extension of my Christian ministry, as the main vehicle and medium for me to impact my generation and beyond, helps to keep me focused.

M25. I have found the writing of poetry one sure discipline if one wants to condense a thousand thoughts, words and feelings into one sentence.

M26. I use writing to de-stress. When I am down and feeling low, I write as a therapy.

M27. When you believe in something, go for it. The monetary gain for me is just surplus, the personal satisfaction cannot be quantified. I wake up each day knowing, as I write, that my thoughts are affecting lives, my talent is not wasted, I am relevant.

M28. I create time for the things that matter and what I believe in. So when friends ask me numerous times how I am able to get time to write, I tell them I don't get time, I make time.

M29. I see my writing as a ministry, because as a friend told me, through these I can reach some who may never be within the confines of a church. Because I see it as such, I invest in it, knowing and believing that through this talent, I can be significant.

M30. I see myself as a distillation plant that takes issues around me - mundane, routine everyday occurrences - as my raw material; then reflects on and processes them, producing various fractions, fit for use by my readers.

M31.   In my works of fiction, the main aim is to project African culture and folklore, which is where I am researching more and more these days. I am in love with our traditional sayings and proverbs and seek to incorporate them more in my stories.

M32.   My pet beef is that, generally, when we talk about arts and entertainment in Ghana, we mean music and dance. Take any newspaper and check out the entertainment pages and you will see what I am talking about. So as a nation, we are paying only lip service to our desire to encourage a reading culture. We are developing our arts and culture only on one leg.

M33.   I don't know where I got this lesson from: 'Learn from the masters, but develop your own voice'.

M34.   My advice to young writers has been to draw an analogy with eating an elephant: no sane person attempts to eat an elephant at once; you do it one bite at a time.

M35.   In terms of self-publishing, it is important to know that self-publishing does not mean shoddy work.

M36.   We have to evolve the practice where our young ones aspire to be novelists, authors, publishers etc. Our entire publishing space is atrophied. And I am being charitable.

We are not feeding it with any oxygen. A near moribund state of affairs.

M37.   An election year is the most likely one in which one can be branded. As a writer, the delicate balance is to remain critical yet unbiased.

M38.   Creatives, including writers, journalists and broadcasters, should get us thinking and reflecting by highlighting the issues on the minds of the general public.

SECTION N
EDUCATION

N1.   The part of Pastor Mensa Otabil's speech about how others supported his education reminded me of this Nigerian proverb: "Those whose palm-kernels were cracked for them by a benevolent spirit should not forget to be humble." Yaw Nsarkoh's article on education is aligned as well. Finally, Manasseh Azure's words came to me, that 'it is difficult to explain the concept of hunger to someone who has never experienced it".

N2.   Many times I heard it asked "How can an educated person say this?" Literacy doesn't guarantee wisdom. I have encountered many literate fools.

N3.   I disagree with any view that affects one's future based on past mistakes. I disagree with the dismissal of girls who commit abortion, from school. I trained as a quality auditor and we were taught that you never penalise twice for the same offense.

N4.   I have issues with the current educational system, never agreed with the direction we took by moving from the O/A Levels to the JHS/SHS system. The middle schools we converted into JSS for preparation to the SHS was shaky and totally unfit for the expectations. So we have created in many communities a system with a very weak middle. My solution then was that we could have asked students to be in the established schools for form one to three, and if they couldn't move on to the purely

139

academic routes after the BECE, they could transfer to the vocational aspects in the same environment. Ask yourself where we are with the reforms. We are back to not just square one, but worse. To confirm my feelings, ask why most of those who can afford it are sending their children to schools that run the O/A Levels. Did you know that some universities in the United Kingdom don't accept our WASSCE certificates as entry requirements anymore?

N5.   A society that is perpetually half rich, half poor is a dangerous one and without the enabler of education, that society is bound to persist and be entrenched.

N6.   The spelling crisis is real.

SECTION O
LEADERSHIP

O1.   As citizens, we should never lose the desire and drive to question. Let's ask questions. Unless we ask 'why' and 'why not', we shall rot in the same way as our society and conditions rot. Let's question our leaders. Let's question their actions and motives. Let's question our peers and challenge them when they do wrong. Let's question ourselves when our peers do better and ask why we can't emulate them and be better. Let us never stop questioning.

O2.   Ghana is not broke. We only have broken leadership.

O3.   Ghana is not broken. We only have leaders with broken spines.

O4.   Seriously, we don't know much about the thought processes of our political leaders. They have written no books, do not write articles and do not write speeches for us to know their minds.

O5.   Our leaders in Abibiman are the greatest practitioners of NATO – No Action, Talk Only. And yet, they are surprised we don't believe all they say.

O6.   Our current leaders were once like you and I - young, full of dreams for the nation, frustrated with the status quo, eager to change the nation, pulsating to see a different

Ghana. May we not become the leaders they are and have our children seeing us in the same light.

O7.   The future belongs to leaders.

O8.   The greatest minds discuss leadership.

O9.   Our leaders love to quote examples of civilized nations only when they want something from us, but forget to quote these examples from the same civilized nations when thinking of what they have to give to, and do for, us.

SECTION P
JOURNALISTS & MEDIA

P1.   How come our media is so adept at sifting only the sensational and mundane out of the news for discussion? Is that tendency a reflection of their own level of understanding and capacity or a reflection of the level of understanding of their listeners and readers?

P2.   I have argued in the past that journalism training should be post-graduate. That way, we could have some specialist journalists as well; for example, journalists who can report on technology, medicine and court proceedings. Otherwise, most reports we will get on such sectors will be done on a foundational knowledge base of oxygen.

P3.   This developing culture of secret recording will lead us into an abyss one day and make us all reluctant to even trust.

P4.   A Journalist of Fortune: worse than a foot soldier. Much, much worse.

P5.   What is journalism as practised in Ghana? Who do we call a journalist? The definition is so loose that it affects the standards as assessed because we have a lot of people who call themselves so who don't deserve the categorisation. My wish is to have journalists setting the agenda and asking serious questions. Questioning and questioning. In a way, like what Chinua Achebe said a writer should do: ask questions and create headaches; he asserted that "it is the duty of a writer to give headaches" and to "write to make people uncomfortable." In *Anthills of the Savannah*, he stated: "Writers don't give prescriptions. They give headaches!" That is the sort of journalism we need to qualify the profession as the fourth estate of the realm and to keep our authorities on their toes. To follow up on issues which are discussed. I asked a question in my book, *I Speak of Ghana*, and still reflect on same: "When will our Ghanaian media stop discussing events and petty squabbles and start discussing ideas and thoughts?"

P6.   How many Ghanaian media outlets sent reporters to cover the Nigerian elections in 2015? Yet we send staff to cover US elections. We have to change our own narrative.

P7.   Businessman or woman - A nebulous term in Ghana. Like that of the journalist.

Connect with The Author Online:

Twitter: @ndamoah

Facebook: http://www.facebook.com/nanaaweredamoah

Instagram: @nanaaweredamoah

Blog: http://nanadamoah.com

Email: ndamoah@yahoo.co.uk